HIGHER

5 Powerful Principles
for Entrepreneurs
to Reinvent Themselves and
Redefine Success to Earn More

SHAYNA M. RATTLER

DISCLAIMER

*This book is dedicated to my "Big Mama," Mary B. Rattler.
Her humor and wisdom will forever guide me.*

*I thank God for the strength and courage to embark on this
journey, and thanks to William Bell for his patience and guidance during the process, and to my family and friends for their
constant support.*

ABOUT THE AUTHOR

Shayna Rattler is a Personal Finance and Certified Business Coach, Author and Speaker. She is the President of Success Unlimited LLC, a business coaching and consulting firm where she empowers business owners and corporate executives to achieve greater life and business success. Shayna has over 10 years of business and management experience that she shares with her clients.

Shayna earned a Bachelor of Science in Occupational Therapy from the University of Tennessee Health Science Center and went on to own and operate a healthcare staffing agency. In addition, she is an experienced real estate investor.

At an early age, Shayna's father taught her the basics of financial literacy. As he stressed the importance of managing her money well, she realized she was a natural at grasping and applying the concepts. Shayna's love of financial training continued to grow, which led to her enrollment in a formal financial literacy training program. There she built on the knowledge started by her father and really perfected the practice of living on a budget.

After her training, Shayna continued to practice the principles she learned from her training and her father. Because of her consistent budgeting practices, *she was able to rid herself of $22,000 in debt in only 8 months!* Now she actively instills those same principles to her own clients.

In addition to her business activities, Shayna is active in her church and community. She serves on the Board of Directors of the National Association of Women Business Owners (NAWBO), on the leadership team of Business Network International (BNI), and is a member of the Greater Memphis Chamber of Commerce. Additionally, she is a participant in the 2012 Executive Program of Leadership Memphis.

She believes giving is a primary principle of financial management and donates a portion of all company proceeds to Big Brother Big Sister of America.

TABLE OF CONTENTS

INTRODUCTION

In the current economy more small businesses are failing than ever before. However, there are a select few that have not only survived, but have thrived. The owners of these select few companies share one thing in common—their level of accomplishment doesn't end there. They continue to look for ways to become the best of the best at what they do. In my opinion, truly successful people are never content. I don't mean that in a negative way; I am simply implying that they are always looking for other ways to stretch themselves and grow. They are constantly in pursuit of their next endeavor.

Does this describe you? If so, you are holding the right resource. I wrote *Higher* for the entrepreneur that is proud of their current achievements and level of success but is looking to enter into their greater purpose in life.

Higher will empower you to take your income and your life to a level beyond what you ever thought possible. In order to transform into this new form of freedom there are some critical personal changes that you must make. You must work from the inside out. Success is not something you pursue; it is something you attract by the person you become. All five principles outlined in this book are generated from within. Before turning to the first page make sure you truly understand and believe that you have everything within yourself that is necessary to become the business owner and own the business you desire!

This practical book will require you to think and act differently. The principles are grassroots in nature, but do not allow yourself not to follow them based purely on their simplistic nature. The outcome is greater results and greater success!

At the end of the book, I have included a bonus section that contains powerful business strategies designed to take your business to the next level. These strategies can be implemented for immediate results.

You will also find a notes section to record any "aha" moments that you have while reading or ideas you wish to implement.

Before we begin, I want to share with you my personal experience with going higher. I graduated from the University of Tennessee Health Science Center with a Bachelor Degree in Occupational Therapy in 2004. After 3 short years of practicing as a therapist, I began a healthcare staffing agency. This business grew rapidly and was extremely financially rewarding. Things were going well and I lived a fairly accomplished life compared to most single, 30 year old women. There was only one problem; something was missing. I felt like there was more to be done. I felt as though my life had more purpose. I spent many nights journaling, praying, and searching for answers.

As I started my business, invested in real estate and began to reduce my debt and build wealth, I frequently advised other aspiring entrepreneurs on the best practices for starting and growing companies. Then it dawned on me; empowering entrepreneurs to live the lives of their dreams by operating successful businesses was my true passion and purpose in life. At that moment I made a decision to become a business coach. I didn't, however, want to be just a business coach; I wanted to be a great business coach. I also wanted my new business venture to be ten times as successful as my staffing agency. I knew if those things were to occur I first had to work on improving myself. I knew that in order to have the business of my dreams, I had to make changes that would move my personal life forward as well. I was determined to go higher. I read books, attended seminars and joined organizations that would transform me into the type of business owner that I would be required to become in order to be prepared for the business I was creating.

The implementation of the five principles described in *Higher* was the driving force behind my transformation. I now want to share those life changing ideas with you. Remember, in order for your business to change and improve, you must change and improve. Let's get started!

Adopt A New Mindset

"We were born to succeed, not to fail." ~ Henry David Thoreau

This first principle is the most important and is the foundation for going higher. The word mindset defined is *a fixed mental attitude or disposition that predetermines a person's responses to and interpretations of situations.* A mindset is a mental attitude. It shapes your actions and your thoughts, as well as how you perceive and respond to events. A common example is whether you see the glass "half empty" or "half full." Your mindset can quickly change what you think, feel, and do. The irony of a mindset is that sometimes you don't know that you're stuck in one until you step out or adopt a different mindset. The trick is knowing how to switch mindsets.

In order to assume control over your circumstances the proper mindset is an absolute must. If your mindset is positive and intentional you will be better equipped to achieve any desired outcome. There are many books and other resources about mindset, and the common theme is usually the same—changing your way of thinking is the only way to get different results. This mantra was likely very necessary to get you to your currently level of success and please understand that it is going to be necessary to yet again adopt a new mindset in order to go higher. William James, known as one of the wisest men in America, said, "The greatest discovery of my generation is that human beings can alter their lives by altering their attitudes of mind." In other words, as you think, so shall you be.

My mindset was once challenged during an internship during Occupational Therapy School. I was assigned to a residential center that housed individuals who were dual-diagnosed with both a substance abuse problem and mental illness. I went into the internship thinking that I would just "get through" my three month commitment and be one step closer to graduation.

I wasn't yet a licensed therapist and didn't expect my role to have a major impact on the residents or myself. Part of my responsibility as a student therapist was to lead group therapy sessions and also conduct individual treatment sessions. I helped my clients deal with issues related to anger management, trust, coping strategies, personal relationships and many other topics. To my surprise the residents responded very well to me. I was told by the center's staff that they had never seen the residents open up to anyone else the way they opened up to me. Each day that I arrived to the center I had a line of residents waiting outside my office door to talk to me.

On the last day of my internship the residents planned a going away lunch where they showered me with gifts they made for me, and they each took turns sharing how I impacted and changed their lives. Of course their comments made me feel great and pulled at my heart strings, but the impact that experience had on my life went much deeper than how I felt emotionally on that day. Spending time with the residents made me realize that I had a deep passion for working with the mentally ill, but more importantly, it made me change my mindset to realize that I should never go into any experience with preconceived notions of what to expect. I am not currently working with the mentally ill population, but one of my long term goals is to open a day center where the homeless, mentally ill can come to receive food, have access to counseling services and community resources.

My friend Shelley Baur, author of Integrity Based Communications, also had a personal experience that resulted in a mindset change that took her life and business to a higher level. In 1994, Shelley was invited to become a facilitation partner for diversity training. Four years after the partnership was formed, Shelley's partner revealed to her that she did not like her when they first met. This shocked Shelley because she prided herself on having excellent communication and relationship building skills. She questioned how she could have missed her partner's feelings and she thought that her usual positive outlook may have blinded her. The wake up call of that experience caused a personal paradigm shift that not only developed her personally, but improved her business as well.

Instead of accepting how things appeared to be on a surface level – her usual positive way of living – she began to look intentionally at the depth and nuanced meaning of her interactions with various people. Ultimately, her mind-set change to a quest for deeper self-awareness led her to formulate an integrity-based communications business model, and use the method and behaviors consistently in her personal life as well. Over the years, her new mindset has continued to advance her business and her life.

> Changing your way of thinking is the only way to get different results.

✦ ✦ ✦

A Paradigm Shift Is Required

Now that you have made the decision to take your life and income to an even higher level of success, you will have to fill your mind with a fresh, new set of thoughts and will have to create new habits. In previous decades it was very common to work at one company for 30 plus years and retire with a watch. It also wasn't unheard of for your children and grandchildren to be hired at that same company and follow a similar path. Those times are over. No longer are the days where getting a good education then a good job equates to stability. With today's current economic state, a good education may mean very little to getting a good job. Even if you get that job, you may find yourself working in a field other than that which you attained a degree, or you may find yourself job hunting in a few short years of landing that dream job.

I personally believe that is the reason for the rapidly growing number of entrepreneurs in America. Entrepreneurs recognize the need for a plan that lasts. They recognize that being average yields nothing more than mediocrity and usually much less. Going higher requires you to be anything but average.

Are there habits in your life that could hinder you from going higher? List them.

1. ....

2. ....

3. ....

4. ....

What action are you going to take to replace those bad habits with good ones?

1. ....

2. ....

3. ....

4. ....

Being average yields nothing more than mediocrity and usually much less.

✲ ✲ ✲

Redefine Persistence

Persistence is one of the character traits that very likely got you to the current level of success that you have attained. It also must be present in order to enter into that next level of success that you are now determined to reach. The key difference will be that you will have to perform harder to reach that level. In fact, be prepared to perform 10 times harder than you did to reach your current level of accomplishment. Not only will your thoughts have to be at a higher level, but so will your actions. This may sound very tiring, and it may be at times. There are going to be days when you will have to keep going even when you don't feel like it, but in order to have what others don't, you will have to do what others won't!

The boxing match of Muhammad Ali vs. Joe Frazier in 1975, commonly known as "The Thrilla in Manila," is a great example of persistence. Muhammad Ali's third fight against his archrival Joe Frazier was a spectacular ending to the long lasting struggle of the two heavyweights who faced each other for a total of 132 minutes in the ring. The "Thrilla in Manila" is considered one of the most brutal and bitter bouts in the history of boxing; it was the only time an Ali – Frazier bout did not last for the scheduled time. After having regained the title against George Foreman in Zaire one year earlier, Ali had successfully defended the belt three times within three months against mostly mediocre opponents. Next he was to face Joe Frazier for the third time to change the record to his favor (Frazier had won the first bout in 1971, Ali prevailed in the rematch three years later).

The bout was important for Ali not only in terms of prestige. He was guaranteed a purse of six million dollars which was twice as much as Joe's and more than Ali had received for the first two fights altogether. As expected, Ali put pressure on Frazier in the beginning, stinging him with jabs and combinations to the head, winning the first rounds. With about a third of the fight over, the tide slowly turned. Ali tired and Joe's punches hit target more often. By round fourteen, Joe's left eye was completely shut so that he was not able to see Ali throwing a right hand any more. In the break before the last round, Frazier's trainer Eddie Futch stopped the fight. Moments after the fight was over, Ali fainted in his corner. No one knows whether he could have resumed the fight. Ali was later quoted that he had been ready to quit if Joe had not. Both Ali and Frazier fought to their absolute limit and maybe beyond.

A similar amount of persistence is necessary to be displayed by the entrepreneur that strives to go higher. But beware; you may lose some friends in the process. When you begin to take your thoughts and actions to a higher level, the average person cannot relate to this type of lifestyle. The things you will be doing will be strange to the average person and you may be criticized. I realize that being criticized doesn't feel good, but it is a sure indicator that you are well on your way to going higher!

Additionally, your personal associations have a direct affect on your energy and growth. The friends and family that embrace this "new and improved you" will be the ones that will continue to accelerate you and you should surround yourself only with these people.

When I was growing up, my grandmother would frequently tell me, "you can't take everyone with you, everywhere you go." I have had to remind myself of that wise quote each time I have found myself "pruning" people from my life or when I have overheard people that were once supportive of me making comments like, "what makes her so special just because she owns a business?"

Remember, extreme success lies beyond the realm of normal action. A high level of persistence will not only get you to the next level you desire, but will prepare you to continue operating at this level throughout your life.

Extreme success lies beyond the realm of normal action.

✲ ✲ ✲

Uplevel Your Life

As you embark on the journey of going higher, become familiar with the term uplevel. Uplevelling is the techniques, ideas, concepts and rituals that will propel your life forward. It consists of the changes that you make from the inside out when you begin to create a life of purpose, empowerment, and abundance. When you begin to uplevel you begin to discover a whole new way to approach your daily life. You will stop surviving and start thriving. When you begin to uplevel you will build a momentum that will make you virtually unstoppable.

In order to go higher, tough decisions will need to be made; decisions that may at first seem to be premature. The primary rule to follow when making decisions is to always make decisions as if you have already arrived at the next level, never from your current level. This is often difficult for some people to do. It is very natural to think that we should set a goal and then take the necessary steps, often in a particular sequence, to reach it. I caution this type of thinking as it is the slowest path to going higher. It is always necessary to think and act as if you have already reached your accomplishments. Never tell yourself that once you meet your goals you will then do this or that.

For example, if hiring additional staff will be necessary for your business to operate successfully at the next level, find a way to fill those positions now. You may want to consider only filling a part-time position, or utilizing a subcontractor for specific projects and specific lengths of time. If dressing differently will be required for your future level of success, begin to purchase and wear those key pieces of clothing now. When setting goals, it is important to write the goals as a statement of accomplishment. For instance, rather than write "I will make $1 million per year," write, "I make $1 million per year."

One of my business mentors and mastermind group leader, Nicole Beurkens, PhD, applied this principle 2 years after starting her clinic in the basement of her home. She took her business to a higher level that may not have occurred had she not been willing to uplevel.

In the beginning, she didn't have a single client; only her expertise and a desire to help children and their families. She also still maintained a full time job in the school system while getting her business off the ground. In the first year of her business she began a summer camp that served 13 children. She quickly realized that there was a need for the service she provided during the school year as well. She added some part-time staff members to her team and began working with clients in addition to her full-time job in the school system.

Two years into this adventure Nicole realized that she wanted to go bigger with her clinic, and that would require a substantial increase in space and staff. Even though she did not yet have the number of clients to require a larger space, she knew it would be needed for the business to grow. She and her husband took a leap of faith and purchased a 3,000 square foot property to house the clinic. She also hired an office assistant on a part-time basis and she and her colleagues began seeing more clients. Two years after moving into the property they again realized that additional space would be needed to grow. They took another leap of faith and invested in a large addition to the building, which doubled the size of their clinic. Over the next year some of her part-time staff moved into full-time status, and she added additional clinical and support staff. At the current time she has a clinic facility that is over 6000 square feet, and employs 13 staff members total.

Looking back, everything looks so well orchestrated and planned, however, at the time it was anything but. Her business has continued to move to the next level as a result of her willingness to implement the vision she has for her company, and to take leaps before she has all the specifics in place. If she had waited to get a bigger space until she had the clients to fill that space, she would probably still be in the basement of her home. Instead, she trusted that moving into the larger space would allow for growth, and it did. Every time she wants to move the business to the next level she realizes that she needs to make decisions as if she is already at that next place, and the details fall into place along the way.

As illustrated in Dr. Beurken's story, when you uplevel your life, you open yourself up for new opportunities both personally and professionally. You will begin to attract people and things that will propel your business and your life higher. Sometimes it may seem as though you have swallowed a magic pill. For example, you may set the intention to connect with a person in the community that you desire to do business with, only to find yourself sitting next to that individual at the next networking event you attend. You will also attract people to your life that will be fully supportive of your career and the person you are becoming.

It was only after I began to uplevel my own life, that I realized that the man of my dreams that I had been searching for had been right before my eyes for over 5 years. One Labor Day weekend, one of my closest friends was going to a restaurant to meet up with the guy she was dating and some of his friends, so I tagged along. This group consisted of about seven men with very different personalities, one of which I immediately connected with.

For several years after we first met, this guy and I fast became friends. At the time, he was married and I had a boyfriend so our relationship with one another was strictly platonic. During this friendship several of my female friends would comment that they thought this guy and I would make a good couple and they thought he was interested in me beyond just being friends. My response was always, "he is a great guy but we're just friends." Years into our friendship he became divorced and I separated from my boyfriend.

He invited me over for dinner one night and we agreed to explore taking our relationship beyond just being friends. There was only one problem—my life was filled with lots of mental clutter and lack of direction. Needless to say, our new definition of a relationship failed.

Over the next year and a half, I spent a lot of time working on myself. I examined what I truly wanted in life and plotted the actions I would take to get there; I focused on the things that really mattered. As a result, it became crystal clear that I had reached a pivotal time in my life and was prepared to go in a higher direction personally and professionally. The question became, was the man that would make this new journey worthwhile and complete willing to give our relationship a second chance?

Thankfully for me, he was willing to do so. As I write this book, we share an amazing relationship that is not only personally fulfilling, but it supports my life as a business owner as well. He is truly my "Million Dollar Man," and I am convinced that had it not been for my mindset change and my decision to uplevel, I would not have been able to attract and receive him into my life.

✲ ✲ ✲

Think Like A Millionaire

If you plan to go higher, not only is it necessary to make decisions as if you have already made it to the next level, it is necessary to think as if you have already made it to the next level. Your thoughts create your reality; the subconscious doesn't know the difference between your thoughts and reality. You have to tell yourself daily that you have already made it to the next level. If you want to go higher you must determine to think on purpose. That is you must consciously and intentionally hold in mind those thoughts that will specifically contribute to your success.

According to Napoleon Hill, our brains become magnetized with the thoughts we hold in our minds. Therefore it is safe to say that our thoughts attract our circumstances. Before you can go higher, you must design your thoughts around an intense desire to achieve greater results until that desire drives you to create definite plans for acquiring it.

In order to create a strong desire, it is extremely important to be able to visualize the outcome. When you are able to visualize what you are attempting to achieve, the likelihood of achieving it becomes greater. So exactly how do you create this desire?

Follow these simple steps to create results-driven thoughts:

1. **Brainstorm on paper.** This will give you absolute clarity about what is important to you, what you want, what you are passionate about and what makes you feel fulfilled.

2. **Be specific about what you want.** Don't just say you want lots of money, a nice home and no stress. Create a picture in your mind of exactly what you want down to the color of the carpet and the list of clients, and then using words draw that picture until your vision is clear.

3. **Make it visible.** Create a vision board of the things you want to have, be, or do. Keep this visualization in a place in your home or office where you will be constantly reminded of your desires.

4. **Focus your energy on what you want.** If you concentrate on all the things you do not want, that is exactly what you will attract more of.

> Our thoughts attract our circumstances.

✥ ✥ ✥

Reinvent Yourself

"Some people dream of success; others wake up and work hard at it." ~ Unknown

Focus On What Really Matters

N ow that your way of thinking is set to go higher, it is now time to focus on your life and habits. In order for your business to change and improve, you must change and improve. With each level of business success, comes a necessary change to your personal life. You must get out of your comfort zone and take different steps to yield different results. For some this is an evolutionary change but for others it will happen immediately.

As a business owner you know it is no secret when I tell you that there is little separation between you and your business. Each is very interrelated and one directly affects the other. When undergoing the process of reinventing yourself, the first thing I encourage you to do is to simplify your life and focus on what really matters. When you first made the decision to go into business for yourself, you likely had a clear, precise reason for doing so. It may have been to provide a comfortable lifestyle for your family or to one day operate a nonprofit agency for inner city youth. While embarking on the journey of entrepreneurship you have likely experienced some ups and downs, had some successes and failures, and hopefully created a desirable lifestyle. You may have very possibly acquired more possessions and traveled more places than you originally imagined.

It is also very likely that you focus much of your time and efforts on the trivial things that occur in business and life rather than on the vital things that assist you in reaching your goals. You have now challenged yourself to transition into an even greater freedom and it is extremely important that before you make that transition that you eliminate obstacles and barriers from your life that have the potential to make your path a more difficult one to travel.

So how exactly, do you simplify your life? If you were to interview 100 entrepreneurs you would likely find that each of their lives are filled with clutter and things that at the end of the day, provide little meaning or substance. These are the things that we should give strong consideration to eliminating or modifying. Now I am not suggesting that you rid your life of all of your worldly possessions and move your loved ones into a tent; I am simply suggesting that you take a hard look at your life and make some minor adjustments. Now that you are going higher and working towards propelling your life and your business to a new level of success, you need to ensure that trivial things will not get in your way or hold you back. I strongly recommend utilizing an accountability partner to help you with these adjustments.

Let me share a personal story with you. When I made the conscious decision to take my own business higher, I did exactly what I am requesting of you. I first looked at who

I was spending my time with, what I spent my time doing, and how those persons and things added to or took away from me reaching my goals. After careful consideration, I realized that there were people in my life that were pulling me down; specifically, my significant other. I was well aware that I was in the wrong relationship long before making the leap to go higher, but it was at that moment that I knew I had had enough.

That individual, although he was a great man, drained me emotionally and physically on a regular basis. He constantly made me feel guilty for taking time to work on my business and even made statements like, "your business is all you care about." Our relationship reached a point that when I achieved a worthy milestone, I felt as though I had to suppress my joy, in fear of the negativity that was likely to follow. I even started lying about my whereabouts if I was at a business meeting simply to "keep the peace." Removing myself from that long-term relationship was one of the most difficult things I have ever had to do, but I realized that my business and my happiness depended on it.

In addition to spending time with the wrong people, I realized that I was spending my days doing activities that would not get me closer to my end goals. I was attending networking events that weren't yielding results and was being let's say, less-than-productive while at home. I immediately stopped attending networking events that weren't producing results, I downgraded my cable service to the lowest level possible, and got rid of everything in my home that I had not used or worn in the previous six months or more. More importantly, I realized that in order to create the business of my dreams and to make more money than I ever had previously, I needed a laser-like focus. In an effort to do so, I made the tough decision to sell my profitable staffing agency in order to completely focus on my coaching business. It was at that point that my business began to go higher.

Now is a good time for you to take inventory of your life and do some spring cleaning. What are you spending your time doing and who are you spending it with? Does it align with going higher?

On the following lines list the things you could live without if you were forced to live in a third world country:

1. ....

2. ....

3. ....

4. ....

5. ....

6. ....

7. ....

8. ....

9. ....

10. ....

Next, list the adjustments you can make in your life if you eliminate or modify some or all of those things:

1. ....

2. ....

3. ....

4. ....

5. ....

6. ....

7. ....

8. ....

9. ....

10. ....

Finally, make a list of the changes you are actually going to make:

1. ....

2. ....

3. ....

4. ....

5. ....

6. ....

7. ....

8. ....

9. ....

10. ....

How will those changes propel your business and life higher?

1. ....

2. ....

3. ....

4. ....

Congratulations, you are now ready to focus on what really matters. More importantly, you have now freed and positioned yourself to attract and openly receive new possibilities and opportunities. The hill you are about to climb is a steep one, but it will be less rocky when what really matters is at the forefront of each day.

Surround Yourself With Success

Reminding you to surround yourself with successful people may seem obvious and not worth mentioning; however, it is vitally important to your ability to go higher. Research has proven that we become most like those that we spend the majority of our time with. Since your business and life is now moving in a different direction, it is going to be critical that the people you are involved with are also experiencing the same level of success or more than you are preparing to achieve. My mentor, Ali Brown, often says, "You can't become the next level of yourself, by yourself."

Your first task is to identify at least three centers of influence that can help take you higher. These are people with a skill set and influence above your own. Your centers of influence will be able to provide you with valuable insights, connect you to important people, and provide you with beneficial feedback. Most importantly, they will provide you with a structure to model.

Find people in your local community or in your industry and pay close attention to what they are doing. There may even be a nationally recognized individual that is living the life you will soon be living. Where do they spend their time, what do they read, and what associations do they belong to? Your goal is to model their behavior and actions. It is not necessary to become their clone, but do not overlook the fact that the same habits that got them to their level of success will be the same habits necessary to take you higher. After you identify a few of these people, get to know them personally if possible. Most of them will be more than happy to share information with you over lunch or become your ongoing mentor. They may even become some of your closest friends.

Here are some examples of where you may find your centers of influence:

1. Your local Chamber of Commerce

2. The Rotary Club

3. Your college alumni

4. Associations/trade groups

5. Professional advisors—CPAs, Attorneys, Insurance Agents

6. Business owners you already know

7. Place of worship

3 Centers of Influence You Plan to Contact:

1. ....

2. ....

3. ....

I advise that you send a letter of introduction to these 3 people and request a meeting. Here is an example of a letter you might send:

Dear Center of Influence:

My name is Shayna Rattler, owner of Success Unlimited. I have been in business for 8 years and am looking to expand my business to offer consulting services to corporations. You have come highly recommended as a respected leader in the community who has experience in servicing corporate clients. It is my belief that to be truly successful it is necessary to seek counsel and surround myself with successful people who are on a path similar to my own.

I would be honored if you would take the time to provide me some advice on strategies that have helped to make your business successful. It would also be of great value to me to receive your feedback on the plans that I have for my business. Further, I would love to learn more about what you do so that I can refer potential clients to you.

Are you available for coffee or lunch during the next two weeks? I can be reached at 123-456-7890 or by email at me@email.com. Thank you in advance for your time and consideration. I look forward to the opportunity.

Sincerely,

Shayna Rattler

✲ ✲ ✲

Seek Counsel

A great way to surround yourself with successful people and provide yourself with a viable sounding board is to join a mastermind group. A mastermind group is two or more people who meet regularly for the purpose of providing mutual support and encouragement to each other. The principle is based on an ancient premise that the combined energies of two or more like-minded persons are many times greater than the sum of the individual energies involved. In a business mastermind group, each participant is able to share successes and receive feedback on challenges or needs occurring within their business. When selecting a mastermind group, make sure the members in the group are smarter than you in some areas and have a business that functions at a higher level than your current business. Do not allow this to intimidate you; these components are essential for your growth.

For significant and sustainable changes to occur in your business and life, you will need someone to turn to for objective feedback and accountability. Human nature doesn't allow for such self-evaluation. To achieve real and lasting breakthroughs, consider hiring a business coach. Even great athletes benefit from someone on the outside to monitor their progress and help them to reach their maximum capabilities. A business coach will challenge you and hold you accountable for changing and going higher.

Take Control Of Your Finances

The purpose of this book is to empower you to unlock greater potential in your business and life, and I would be doing you a disservice if I didn't encourage you to address your personal finances. If you are like many entrepreneurs, you have acquired some personal debt to start and grow your business. As the owner, you are also responsible for overseeing or managing the budget and financial statements for the business.

After applying the principles in this book you will be in a position to drastically increase your income. If you haven't already, take the time to get your personal finances in order. Be sure to be living on a budget, save consistently, decrease your consumer debt, increase your credit score, invest for future wealth, and make giving a priority. If necessary consult a personal finance coach to assist you. I offer a resource in the Appendix to help you do this on your own.

Do A Reality Check

"The secret of success is to do the common things uncommonly well." ~ John Rockefeller

magine this… you are walking along a dirt road with the goal of getting to the other side of town. Along your way, you run into a big brick wall. This wall is completely blocking your path and it stops you dead in your tracks.

What do you do? Do you give up and go home? Do you just sit there and hope the wall will eventually disappear? Do you push against it to try and move it with force? Or do you overcome the obstacle by finding a way to get around it?

Our limiting beliefs are like big brick walls blocking us on our path to freedom, wealth, and success. We all have them; it's just a matter of learning how to work through them when they arise. When you near the point of going higher, it is common for limiting beliefs to creep in. It happens to even the best of us. I realize that your perception often becomes your reality, but the key is not to allow those beliefs to paralyze you and prevent you from moving forward. Often these beliefs are invisible to us. When present, these beliefs can control your thoughts and behaviors and can prevent you from taking your business and your life higher. For example, if you have the false belief that mistakes and failure are bad, then you'll avoid many growth and learning experiences because you have to be willing to fail in order to build new skills.

> # Our limiting beliefs block us on our path to freedom, wealth, and success.

Where do these beliefs come from? Many limiting beliefs get instilled during childhood, but that isn't always the case. The pattern is that your mind drew false generalization based on one or more specific events. It assigned questionable meanings to those events, and those interpretations are disempowering you. As a result your mind blocks you from taking certain actions, even though the actions may be reasonable and intelligent choices.

Complete the following statements to discover what your limiting beliefs may be:

I am too _____

I am not _____

I have a fear of _____

I would be more successful if only _____

As a business owner I can not _____

My biggest challenge is _____

If I have a setback I _____

I may need help with _____

Under pressure I _____

I struggle with _____

You may be aware of some of your limiting beliefs, but awareness of them isn't necessarily enough to keep them from operating in your life. When it comes to ingrained limiting beliefs, these can be a bit harder to change, but if you are going to be successful at reaching a higher level, you must learn how to get around these beliefs and continue along your path with much more enthusiasm, determination, and motivation than ever before. There are several things you can do to shift toward more empowering beliefs:

1. Stop identifying with the belief. In other words, do not define yourself based on what you believe. For example, if you think you're not creative, you'll see yourself as someone who just wasn't born with that ability.

2. Determine if the belief is perception or reality. Is there rock solid evidence that this belief is true? It is very likely that there is no real proof.

3. Reverse the belief. Ask yourself if the opposite of your limiting belief can be true, if not more true. For instance, if your limiting belief is that you don't have value, reverse it and say to yourself, "I do have value." Now look for ways that prove that.

It is likely that you will have some internal resistance to this at first, but it is critical that you work through it and move forward. You will not be able to go higher if you don't. If you do not address these limiting beliefs they will continue to limit your personal and professional growth. If necessary, consult with a professional to help with this area.

Take Massive Action

"Success doesn't come to you, you go to it ~ Marva Collins

Now that your mindset is set to go higher and you are properly positioned for success, you must dig a little deeper. It's time to shift your actions into higher gear. This is the key element of going higher. Success is less about ideas and more about implementation. More importantly, success is about taking massive action, especially at the next level. The act of taking action, in and of itself, is a magnet for wealth and opportunity.

Remember, a step in the wrong direction is better than staying in the same spot. Once you're moving, you can always course correct if necessary, but your auto-guidance system can't guide you if you are standing still. It is not, however, necessary to have things perfectly in place before you begin to take action of going to a higher level. Just start now! Begin each day by making a list of things that you will do in order to achieve greater and higher results.

Leapfrog Your Way To The Top

One of the best things about being an entrepreneur is freedom. One of the freedoms you have as an entrepreneur is the ability to determine how your business will grow. It is entirely up to you how fast or slow you take your business to the next level. In order for your business and income to reach a higher level than it is now, you must dare to excel. It doesn't take any more effort to dream a big dream than it does to dream a small one so you may as well aim high.

When you first began your business it was probably wise to take small, incremental steps. Now your business is successful and you desire to take it to the next level. Recognize that it is not necessary to climb the ladder of success rung by rung. By that I mean there is no need to follow the strategy that "before I can do that, I must first do this." I'm not talking about taking unbridled risk but I am suggesting that you have the courage to effectively advance in large steps in the least amount of time.

Dr. Beurkens' story previously mentioned in the uplevel section is a great example of taking leaps toward

going higher. She didn't wait until she outgrew her existing space and exceeded the capacity of her current staff
before making the decision to move into a larger space and
hire more staff. Her business grew rapidly by taking large
steps.

> It is not necessary to climb the ladder
> of success rung by rung.

✧ ✧ ✧

Act Like A Millionaire

Not only is it necessary to think as though you have already achieved the next level of success as millionaires do, you must also act as though you have achieved it. If you look around you, there are examples everywhere of people that are living extraordinary lives as the result of owning highly profitable businesses. There are also stories of people that make fortunes working only a few hours per week.

I don't give these examples to place emphasis on material things, but rather I give them to place emphasis on the fact that these things are only possible with immense action. The same level of action required to obtain these results must be sustained. This is not the sort of thing that you do only to gain momentum. Taking massive action will take you higher and those same levels of action will be required to stay at that level and beyond. You may need to implement strategies such as starting your day earlier and ending it later, or calling 5 more prospects than you typically call per day.

If you take a look at the businesses of highly successful entrepreneurs you will notice a common theme; they have systems in place. You must have a system in place for every function of your business. Robert Kiyosaki, successful entrepreneur, investor, and author, says that if you can not leave your business for an extended amount of time and return to find it functioning as well, if not better than when you left, that you do not actually have a business. You have a job. Systems are what allow you to do so.

As I was writing this book, I took a week long vacation with my family and my business continued to run. Not once did I call my office or even check my email. I felt comfortable doing so because I have created a business that is systems-dependent and not owner-dependent. I returned to find things not as I left them, but better. While I was away, my team created new ideas to generate clients, newsletters went out, and clients were served.

Set Over The Top Goals

Much has been written about goal setting. We all know that goals must be measurable, specific, etc., but the goals that you set for going higher must be slightly different than your average goal. Your goals for the new stage of your business and life must be set beyond what you have ever thought possible. Now is the time to think big! The objective is not to just forecast a future that you think is attainable but to actually set goals that allow you to create the future you desire. For each goal, take your first inclination and multiply it. This is the only way to set the stage for going higher. Again, it is not enough to want it; you have to create it.

There is a famous quote that says, "A person may aim high and hit low, but he never hits high if he aims low." In the world of business it is dangerous to aim low. It sets you up for failure, slows success, sabotages true happiness, causes depression, suppresses hopes and dreams, and literally causes some people to be physically unhealthy. It is impossible to succeed at going higher if you aim low.

So, why do so many people choose to aim low at all? I think it's because of one or more of these 3 reasons:

1. It seems too hard to aim high.
2. They don't think aiming high is attainable.
3. They don't know how to get there.

A perfect example of a person who aimed high can be found in the story of Aimee Mullins. She set her sights high and it paid off. Aimee was born with a rare disease and had both of her legs amputated below the knee when she was a year old. In college she competed against well-bodied athletes in track and field events and also competed in the Paralympics in Atlanta in 1996. Aimee went on to become an actress and model. She easily could have slipped into depression and allowed her disability to define her. Instead she defined herself and went higher.

Focus On The Vision

*"To guarantee success, act as if it
were impossible to fail."* ~ Dorothea Brande

Have A Big Why

There is surely a reason for your desire to go higher. Obviously the higher you go, the more your income increases, but for most entrepreneurs the desire is fueled by more than money. If you don't have a big enough "why," now is the time to stop and think about it. What is your greater purpose in life? What would you do with your time if money were no object? Is there a charity or cause that you are passionate about?

When you have a meaningful purpose you create an unstoppable energy that will propel your thoughts and efforts each day. I encourage you to post your "why" where you can see it daily. On the days when you feel like throwing in the towel or taking the easier route by settling for your existing level of accomplishments, glance over at your "why" to remind yourself of its significance and to motivate you into taking massive action.

For example, here is my why:

I need my business to create enough income and eventually passive income so I can:

1. Create a legacy for my future grandchildren

2. Donate $50,000 per year to Big Brother Big Sister of America

3. Open and operate a day center for the homeless, mentally ill and not need a salary from it

4. Fund an after school and summer program for the youth of my church

List your Why here:

____

____

____

✲ ✲ ✲

Let Your Vision Guide You

It is extremely important not to get caught up in the how. The specific strategies you implement to go higher may be very similar to the ones you implemented to obtain your current level of achievement. It is more important to focus on your vision than the vehicle that will take you there. When you combine your energy and passion with your vision, you will attract the vehicle.

What is your vision? If it took you more than 10 seconds to answer, you need to develop it. Spend time on this; be sure it is big and clear. Now is the time to be bold. You deserve it. You've worked hard to get where you are and you've earned the right to go higher. If you follow a direct line to your vision, your income and the vehicle to get there will come.

For example, here is the vision for my business:

I want my coaching and consulting firm to be the premier resource for stimulating small businesses across the country and empowering women to create the lives of their dreams through business ownership. I would like our company headquarters to include our offices, meeting, and conference space. I would also like to have an on-site resort space that includes sleeping rooms, a formal dining room, auditorium, swimming pool and lake to hold yearly retreats for business owners.

List your Vision here:

____

____

____

✲ ✲ ✲

Follow Your Inner Energy

Would you rather be pulled forward easily to the next level or have to push your way there? I am certain your answer wasn't push. There is a way to go higher with ease. One of the easiest ways to uplevel your business and your life is to gain guidance from a higher power. Your higher power may be God, spirit, or universe, whatever. Now that you have made the conscious decision to take your income and your life to the next level you will likely have an increased demand for courage and faith.

I've mentioned before that there will be few people in your life, maybe not even your spouse, who will completely understand your transformation. When fear or doubt creeps in, you must have somewhere to turn. Attracting the new life you want is not enough; it is just the beginning. Limiting beliefs may creep back in, but you experience a tremendous amount of growth when you are uncomfortable.

There is a reason a small percentage is not at the level you are striving to reach. The IRS states that less than 10% of the United States earns more than $100,000 per year. That said, you may only have yourself and your higher power to lean on when putting your thoughts and feelings into action to lead you toward your end result.

Make time each day to connect to your source of higher power and make a commitment to live under its guidance. By doing so you will better understand the processes and phases you will go through as you step into the new version of you. If you listen to this guidance your income and success will continue to grow. It is when you direct your inner energy correctly and then take action that the increase in income comes and before you know it, YOU ARE HIGHER!!!

Putting It All Together

ow that you are equipped to go higher, I want to give you a deeper understanding of the characteristics of the "new you" and provide you with some fun and practical ways to apply the principles to your business and life. It will not only help you better understand yourself, but will also make you more aware of potential aspects of your life that you may need to further address to be more effective in life and business. This information will empower you to embrace your new style so that you will become happier, wiser, and freer.

As a business owner at a higher level, there is one word that describes you: COURAGEOUS! As you continue forward on your courageous journey, keep the following in mind:

Your greatest challenge: With such a big vision and fire in your belly you can feel overwhelmed and wonder how you will get it all done. Like a giant oak tree, trust that you have deeply planted roots and no matter what happens you will find a way to succeed.

Your greatest opportunity: By staying positive and knowing your priorities you can achieve anything. Be in charge of your body, your time, and your mind so you can stay focused upon your big target.

Your way of communicating: You focus on the results first, and want others to present the conclusion or outcome to you at the beginning. You also keep communication succinct and to the point, without offering too many options.

Strengths		Areas for Growth
Fast paced, quick thinker		May make decisions too fast
Not afraid to take risks		Competitive nature can bring out worst
Hard to intimidate		Dislike of detail can lead to errors
Focus on action and end result		Impatient with others who can't keep up
Decisive		Can be quick to judge others
Natural leader		Have a tendency to dominate
Brings things into use		Can come across as intimidating
Apply experience to problems		Strong need for control

The Many Hues Of Higher

It has been proven that the human brain seeks patterns. It is wired to look for similarities and to resonate with those. Without being aware of it, we look for things, like the clothes we choose to wear, that connect with those patterns. I have chosen a color to represent each of the principles in the book. The color assigned to each is based on the psychology behind each color. There is nothing scientific or exact about the correlation between the color and the corresponding principle; it is simply a fun way to utilize the book and remember the principles.

As you explore ways to apply each principle to your business and your life, allow each color to remind you of what you should be focusing on. For example, you can start your day by telling yourself, "this will be a red day," or as you take a specific action you can refer to it as a "green moment." Look for patterns and habits already in your daily life and figure out ways to incorporate the corresponding color to those habits.

Here are additional examples of how to make the most of each principle:

1. Decorate your home or office with colored accent pieces.

2. Add fresh flowers or a bowl of that color fruit to your desk.

3. Use a colored poster board to list the changes you plan to make to simplify your life. Hang this list in your office where you will see it daily.

4. Spend 15 minutes per day reflecting on that day's successes and name it "X-Color Time."

5. Add an article of clothing or piece of jewelry of that color to your wardrobe.

6. Journal your daily successes in that specific colored ink.

7. Burn colored candles in your office.

8. Print your vision or your why and display it in a colored picture frame.

9. Use colored file folders.

10. Change your computer's screensaver to a picture of that color.

11. Display artwork of that color.

12. Use colored highlighters.

13. Use colored golf balls.

Adopt A New Mindset = Orange—The color orange represents happy and energetic times. It also is a symbol of ambition and a new dawn in attitude.

Reinvent Yourself = Green—The color green represents growth, nature, money, and good luck.

Do A Reality Check = Yellow—The color yellow represents happiness, optimism, and creative thoughts.

Take Massive Action = Red—The color red is a symbol of life, energy, movement, and excitement. It draws attention and the human eye looks there first.

Focus On The Vision = Blue—The color blue represents dependability, wisdom, and loyalty.

Powerful Business Strategies
For Immediate Results

ow that you have transformed into a *Higher* business owner, here are a few practical strategies you can apply to your business to take it higher. Included is some of the same advice I give to my private coaching clients to kick up their revenue.

Be A Strategic Owner

You should run your business; it should not run you. Be sure to put people and systems in place so the business can function practically without you. Your business should not depend upon your presence, problem-solving, and over-seeing for its daily survival. If it does, you business doesn't work, you do.

Master Your Time

Use your time wisely. Figure out what your time is worth and complete the tasks and projects that only you can complete. Every other task should be automated, delegated or deleted. Remember, you cannot go higher doing $10.00 per hour jobs.

Use Effective Marketing

Traditional forms of marketing no longer work. There are only 3 ways to increase your income—increase your number of clients/customers, increase your average transaction value, and increase the frequency of repurchase. Consider using email newsletters, Send Out Cards, direct mail, and social media to stay in touch with your ideal client.

Form Strategic Alliances

A strategic alliance can look one of two ways. A strategic alliance may be a person or organization that is targeting the same market as your organization, or it may be an organization that conducts a similar type of business as your organization. In the first example, the relationship is beneficial to your company because the other organization can refer clients/customers to you or can make introductions to your ideal client/customer. In the latter example, a mutual agreement may be made to do business together on a specific project in order to create scalability for the two smaller companies. Either way, it is important to nurture and stay in constant contact with strategic alliance partners.

Have A Website That Sells

Your website should be more than a static brochure; it should be a lead generating tool. The goal of your website is to be found and to provide great content that engages the buyer. Be sure to:

- Have a purpose and strategy
- Create good content

- Use keyword-rich text to rank high in the search engines
- Have a clear call to action such as a newsletter sign up or call for a consultation

Have Multiple Streams Of Income

Your business should strive to have unique offerings in different mediums and at different price points. If you are a service company you may want to consider also offering information products. If you are a product-based company you may consider also offering a service that accompanies your product lines. When possible, also have offerings available both on and off line.

Sell Authentically

There is a craft to learning to sell without being "salesy." The goal is to bridge the gap for your client/customer. In order to keep your sales authentic remember to:

- Keep the client's/customer's needs in mind
- Keep rapport throughout
- Be curious
- Keep it natural

Be A Powerful Networker

When considering to join a networking group, ensure that the primary objective of the group is business related and not a social event. Once you find the appropriate group, remember that the key to receiving key referrals is to give key referrals. Be on the lookout for potential prospects and referral sources for your business. To get the most out of a networking group, become part of the leadership team.

Receive weekly tips, resources, and other information to grow your business in our **FREE** email newsletter, *Success Unlimited*. Sign up on our website at www.businesscoachmemphis.com.

What Is Business Coaching?

- Business coaching has exploded into a $3 billion industry, as business owners increasingly seek professionals to help them achieve greater financial success as well as personal balance and fulfillment, particularly in a tough economy.

- Business owners and executives are rapidly realizing the importance of coaching services as the coaching industry grows at a 30 percent annual rate. Owners experience a minimum of 3x-5x return on investment.

- Simply put, business coaching is the art and science of counseling entrepreneurs to overcome obstacles that keep them from reaching optimal success in business and in life.

- Business coaching is recession resistant. It is needed in good times and bad.

- In good economies, small business owners want to aggressively grow their businesses. In tough economies, they want to hold on and not lose everything they have created.

Reasons To Hire A Business Coach

1. Because you want to make more money (profit) in your business.

2. Because you are sick of feeling like your business is in charge of *you*.

3. Because you want some time back to spend on yourself (instead of your business).

4. Because bringing someone else into your business, to challenge you, to push you, and to inspire you again, might just take you somewhere better.

Further Guidance

For some of you this book will be enough to guide your path to a higher level of success. Others of you will want to go deeper. Additional coaching is available to empower you to achieve greater success and balance in your business and personal life. Take advantage of these proven, money back guaranteed offers. Visit our website at www.businesscoachmemphis.com or call us at 901-328-8842 for additional information.

A. Strategic Business Owner—Ongoing 6 month coaching program designed to enhance your mindset, focus, results, balance, and profits. Includes one group workshop per month and one individual phone session per month.

B. Strategic Leader—3 month coaching program designed for corporate executive teams to enhance their mindset, focus, results, balance, and profits.

C. Business Tune Up—One ½ day strategy session designed to provide you with immediate results. Leave with a detailed action plan to grow your business.

D. Roadmap to Financial Freedom—Home study course designed to help you take control of your personal finances at your own pace.

E. Free, no obligation 20 minute consultation to explore solutions for success.

Make Your Next Event A Success By Having Shayna As The Speaker

Are you looking for a speaker for your association, meeting, conference, or just need that extra push for your employees? Shayna Rattler is a vivacious speaker who provides insight on a wealth of topics. She goes beyond the traditional motivational speaker by combining inspiration with suggested action steps for audiences. Through her dynamic presentations, Shayna draws on her personal experiences and excellence to share with audiences those essential elements that comprise her vision of entrepreneurial success, leadership, vision, and life. In every talk, Shayna draws upon her business, personal wisdom and know-how combined with industry facts and information to help your audience both emotionally identify with the intended message and rationalize the need to alter behaviors, modify strategies, or feel transformed.

The following are samples of the talks Shayna offers. Other topics may be available upon request.

7 Critical Steps to Becoming a Strategic Business Owner: How to Double Your Profits with Half of the Effort

Obtain greater achievement, fulfillment, and success by learning to think and act differently as a business owner. Elevate your performance and results by working smarter, not harder while maintaining a healthy balance in your life. In the end you will earn more money, work less, and enjoy a richer, more fulfilling life.

Turning Time into Money: Productivity and Time Mastery Strategies to Drive Success in Your Business and Life

Entrepreneurship is truly about turning time into money. Learn to master your time, and ultimately your success by shifting your priorities in order to get the right things done to move your business forward fast. You will also learn to effectively use systems, tools, and your environment to stop being busy and start being productive. The end result is making more money and achieving your best results while still having energy and a life.

5 Powerful Principles to Take Your Business Higher

Work from the inside out to transform your business and your life into a greater purpose. Learn to redefine success, reinvent yourself and take your business to the next level, while earning more money than you ever thought possible. You will learn how to change your way of thinking to get greater results, focus on the things that really matter, create habits that accelerate growth in the least amount of time, and how to attract the vehicle that leads to your vision.

The Profit Puzzle: Take Control of Your Finances to Accelerate Business Growth

Your solid foundation for building a profitable business begins with the ability to effectively manage your personal finances. Learn to implement new behaviors and strategies to make running your business more manageable. Also learn to grow your business without creating huge personal debt.

*All topics can be tailored to meet the specific needs of your event.

"Shayna is a dynamic, engaging and authentic speaker. She brings a warmth and presence to the stage that people can relate to and she always shares relevant information, which can be applied immediately to take your life and business to the next level" ~ Keith Thomas

Higher

Notes/Aha Moments

78

www.ingramcontent.com/pod-product-compliance
Lightning Source LLC
Chambersburg PA
CBHW071242170526
45165CB00003B/1207